The Christian  Pocket Guide

The Christian Counsellor's Pocket Guide

SELWYN HUGHES

KINGSWAY PUBLICATIONS
EASTBOURNE

Copyright © Selwyn Hughes 1977, 1982

First published by Crusade for World Revival 1977
This revised edition published 1982
Reprinted 1983, 1985, 1986, 1988, 1991, 1994

All rights reserved
No part of this publication may be reproduced or
transmitted, in any form or by any means, electronic
or mechanical, including photocopying, recording, or any
information storage and retrieval system, without
permission in writing from the publisher.

ISBN 0 86065 153 3

Unless otherwise indicated, biblical quotations
are from the Authorized Version (crown copyright).

TLB = The Living Bible
© Tyndale House Publishers 1971

PHILLIPS = The New Testament in Modern English
by J. B. Phillips, © J. B. Phillips 1958.

GNB = Good News Bible
© American Bible Society 1976

Produced by Bookprint Creative Services
P.O. Box 827, BN21 3YJ, England for
KINGSWAY PUBLICATIONS
Lottbridge Drove, Eastbourne, E. Sussex BN23 6NT
Printed in Great Britain

Be sure to use the abilities God has given you.... Keep a close watch on all you do and think. Stay true to what is right and God will bless you and use you to help others.

1 Timothy 4:14–16 (TLB)

A counsellor?
... Who? ... Me?

Helping people with their problems is not just the task of professional counsellors—it is the commission of every Christian also. Whether we realize it or not almost all of us are involved in counselling situations every day of our lives. A friend has a problem in his marriage; a neighbour has lost a loved one; a relative has discovered that she has cancer; a son or daughter has to be challenged about their unacceptable behaviour—all these are counselling situations demanding insight, sympathy and personal concern.

You do not need to be a professional counsellor, or to have received specialized training, in order to help people with their problems. It is true, of course, that some people are supernaturally gifted by God for this purpose, as explained in Romans 12:6, 8: 'Through the grace of God we have different gifts... and if our gift be the stimulating of the faith of others let us set ourselves to it' (Phillips). This gift of 'stimulating the faith of others' is the God-given ability to help uncover and resolve the deep problems which hinder Christians in their spiritual growth and progress towards spiritual maturity. You might now be saying, 'Well, I'm not conscious of having a special gift in counselling, so that lets me off.' It doesn't! Even though you may not have a particular spiritual gift for dealing with problems in depth, every Christian is commanded by God to have a practical and sacrificial concern for others. James tells us, 'Now what use is it, my brothers, for a man to say he "has faith" if his actions do not correspond with it?' (Jas 2:14 Phillips). A similar thought is expressed in Philippians 2:4—'Don't just think about your own affairs, but be interested in others, too, and in what they are doing' (TLB). In 1 Thessalonians 5:11 we are told to 'encourage each other and build each other up' (TLB), and in Galatians 6:2 we are commanded to 'share each other's troubles and problems, and so obey our Lord's command' (TLB).

The New Testament encourages every Christian to assume the responsibility for each other's spiritual development, and it is to help towards that end that this booklet has been compiled. Recent studies have shown that Christian laymen and non-professional counsellors are sometimes more effective in helping people with their problems than those with long years of specialized training. A survey conducted by Robert Karkhuff on the results of a research into comparisons between professional and lay counsellors indicated that the counsellees of lay counsellors improved as well as (and in some cases better than) those of the professionals. This conclusion does not invalidate the need for specialized training in counselling, but it does show that those who are untrained and have a genuine desire to help others can bring about great changes in the lives of those whom they counsel.

O. H. Mowrer, ex-president of the American Psychological Association, in his book *The Crisis in Psychiatry and Religion*, has openly challenged the view that only professionally trained counsellors should handle serious problems. He claims that Christian laymen can bring a healing spiritual dimension into the lives of those who are seriously troubled and disturbed that no secular counsellor or therapist could match.

The question is often asked, 'How does Christian counselling differ from secular counselling?' In two ways: (1) Christian counselling is largely *directive*, as opposed to the non-directive approach of secular counsellors; and (2) it makes great use of the Bible. Much of modern-day counselling encourages the counsellee to look within himself for the solutions to his problem. Christian counselling seeks to bring the principles of God's word, the Bible, to bear upon human problems, and there are times in the counselling process when the best thing you can do for the counsellee is to read him what God says about the matter in the Scriptures. Christian counselling is therefore *telling people, with deep compassion and genuine love, what God requires of them.*

We are told in 2 Timothy 3:16 that the breath of God has gone into the compilation of the Bible and it is, therefore, a *God-breathed book.* 'All scripture is given by inspiration (or the breath) of God, and is profitable for doctrine, for reproof, for correction, for instruction in righteousness.' We see also that the breath of God has gone into the creation of man, 'And the Lord God...breathed into his nostrils the breath of life; and man became a living soul' (Gen 2:7). The same breath that went into the making of man has gone into the making of the Bible, for it was God's intention that the Scriptures should become the reference book for man's continued spiritual and psychological development on this earth. Along with the product (man) God has provided a *Manufacturer's Handbook* (the Bible) which contains all the principles necessary to a happy and successful life in this world and the world to come.

Caution

Finally, a word of caution. One of the most important aspects of counselling, whether it is dealing with problems in depth or simply sharing spiritual advice, is to know when to refer. This is a matter that cannot be too strongly emphasized. You should always be ready to refer the person you are counselling to someone more experienced than yourself whenever you feel that the problem is outside the limits of your own insight or experience. Watch out for the following signs which tell you to consider introducing the person you are counselling to a minister, or an appropriate professional person:

- when a person has severe depression, or remains suicidal even after your best efforts to help;

- when you lack the physical or spiritual stamina to deal with the problem;

- when the person arouses strong feelings of dislike in you;

- when the person requires medical attention;

- when the person has serious financial difficulties.

They will not feel rejected when referring them to someone else if you preface your remarks with the statement, 'I want to help you, but your problem is beyond the limits of my ability and experience. I would like therefore to introduce you to someone whose experience is greater than mine in this matter and who will, I feel sure, be able to help you much better than I can.'

May God bless you as you give yourself to the task of bringing about a spiritual change in the lives of those whom God leads you to counsel.

The Christian Counsellor's
Pocket Guide

Section A

The first section deals with sixteen problems which are often raised by Christians, and contains suggestions on how to deal with these difficulties, together with Scripture references that relate to the particular situation. You will soon discover that as you begin to use these simple suggestions, you will be able to expand on them and build up additional insights and Scripture references. Remember always to pray with a brother or sister who is in difficulty: this will help more than you could ever imagine.

Although at one time the major responsibility for counselling and helping Christians with their spiritual problems rested upon ministers and members of the clergy, something of a revolution is at present taking place within the body of Christ as believers are beginning to see the truth of *every-member ministry*.

More and more Christians are realizing that every Christian has a ministry within the body of Christ, and part of that ministry is to encourage and support each other in times of personal trouble or difficulty. 'God has put together the body in such a way that extra honour and care are given to those parts that might otherwise seem less important. This makes for happiness among the parts, so that the parts have the same care for each other that they have for themselves. If one part suffers, all parts suffer with it, and if one part is honoured, all the parts are glad' (1 Cor 12:24–26 TLB).

Christian problems

Bible References

Whatsoever things are true, whatsoever things are honest...just...pure...lovely...of good report... think on these.

(Phil 4:8)

Set your affection on things above, not on things on the earth.

(Col 3:2)

Unto the pure all things are pure.

(Tit 1:15)

Let this mind be in you, which was also in Christ Jesus.
(Phil 2:5)

Thou wilt keep him in perfect peace, whose mind is stayed on thee: because he trusteth in thee.

(Is 26:3)

Stand in awe, and sin not: commune with your own heart.

(Ps 4:4)

Meditate upon these things; give thyself wholly to them.
(1 Tim 4:15)

I am troubled by wrong thoughts

Be careful to point out to the person who has this problem that wrong thoughts in themselves are not sin. 'We can't stop the birds flying over our heads,' said one theologian, 'but we can stop them building nests.' Evil thoughts only become sin when the mind fondles them, nurtures them and continues to hold on to them. Encourage the person concerned not to repress the thoughts, that is, push them down into the subconscious, but to lift them up to God in *praise*. Though at first this might sound like a very unspiritual technique, it does in fact work. For if we push wrong thoughts into our subconscious mind and try to bury them there, these thoughts are not buried dead—they are buried *alive*. They continue to work in the subconscious in different ways. So we lift them to God. But why praise God for evil thoughts? Isn't that going too far? See how this principle works in the life of a Christian familiar with the technique. One day he is going down the road thinking of nothing in particular when a wrong thought enters his mind. Instantly he brings that wrong thought to God in an attitude of praise. He says, 'Thank you, Lord, for this wrong thought, because through it my attention is being drawn to you; it has become a stepping stone which is making me more aware of your presence and your love in my life.' If the person can also be encouraged to spend a little time in reading the Scripture as well, then wrong thoughts will serve to deepen one's fellowship and communion with the Lord. You can be sure that if Satan is responsible for sending the wrong thoughts, he will soon give up, because the last thing he wants to do is divert a believer's attention to his heavenly Father.

Bible References

When my heart is overwhelmed: lead me to the rock that is higher than I.

(Ps 61:2)

Consider him that endured such contradiction of sinners.

(Heb 12:3)

Men ought always to pray, and not to faint.

(Lk 18:1)

When the enemy shall come in like a flood, the spirit of the Lord shall lift up a standard against him.

(Is 59:19)

Casting all your care upon him; for he careth for you.
(1 Pet 5:7)

Even when we are too weak to have any faith left, he remains faithful to us.

(2 Tim 2:13 TLB)

For [God] hath said, I will never leave thee, nor forsake thee.

(Heb 13:5b)

I am easily upset

A person with this problem needs to be shown that it is not so much what happens to us but what we do with it that matters. Share the truth which is found in James 1:2–3 (Phillips) and point out that according to these verses there are two ways we can take in responding to our problems: (1) to resent them as intruders; and (2) to welcome them as friends. We either respond to trials and difficulties with resentment and say, 'Why should this happen to me?' or we respond to them with praise and say, 'God is sovereign. He would allow nothing to take place in my life unless he sees that it can be worked to good, so I will accept this problem as a friend, put out the "Welcome" mat and watch what God will do.' When we can learn to accept all of life's problems with praise, this makes our spirits creatively objective, enabling us to use problems for the development of our characters and the improvement of our personalities. Point out to the person that according to Romans 8:28–29 God screens every event that takes place in our lives and permits only what he can use. If we respond to life's situations with gratitude, rather than a grudge, we enable God by our co-operation to achieve his highest purpose in us, which is using the problems and irritations that beset us to shape our lives more closely to the image of his Son. People become upset when they fail to see their lives from God's point of view. Your task as a counsellor here is to help them see their difficulties as tools in God's hands, producing greater character and Christlikeness.

Bible References

Study to shew thyself approved unto God, a workman.
(2 Tim 2:15)

And beside this, giving all diligence, add to your faith virtue; and to virtue knowledge.

(2 Pet 1:5)

God has given each of us the ability to do certain things well.

(Rom 12:6 TLB)

Always keep your conscience clear.
(1 Tim 1:19 TLB)

If we confess our sins, he is faithful and just to forgive us our sins, and to cleanse us from all unrighteousness.
(1 Jn 1:9)

Thy word have I hid in mine heart, that I might not sin against thee.

(Ps 119:11)

Put on the new man, which after God is created in righteousness and true holiness.

(Eph 4:24)

I am not growing spiritually

There are four major reasons why Christians fail to grow. You will need to cover them one by one as follows. (1) *Failure to maintain a clear conscience.* If any sin, or violation of God's word, is not dealt with immediately, then it lies in the heart and festers. Probe gently to see if the person can remember violating God's word in any way, and once something is discovered begin to put it right. (2) *Neglect of personal prayer.* Every Christian needs to spend some time alone with God every day. If this is not done or the *quiet time* is scamped, then it will not be long before spiritual dryness sets in. Ask the person whether he or she has a daily appointment with God in prayer. (3) *Lack of daily Bible reading.* In order to grow, a Christian must have a daily intake from the word of God, the Bible. The word of God is a Christian's nourishment. Failure to feed one's spirit with the truths that flow out of Scripture will result in spiritual apathy and indifference. (4) *No clear understanding of one's place in the body of Christ.* Many Christians become frustrated and fail to grow because they have never discovered their place in the body of Christ. Every Christian is designed by God to fit into a special place in his body, the church. Examine Romans 12:6–8 to see the seven basic gifts that contribute to the growth and health of Christ's body. *Every* Christian has at least one of these gifts. Help the person discover and develop it. (For a fuller explanation of this point, see *How to Live the Christian Life* by Selwyn Hughes.)

Bible References

Be honest in your estimate of yourselves, measuring your value by how much faith God has given you.

(Rom 12:3 TLB)

God has given each of us the ability to do certain things well.

(Rom 12:6 TLB)

You saw me before I was born and scheduled each day of my life before I began to breathe.

(Ps 139:16 TLB)

Man looketh on the outward appearance, but the Lord looketh on the heart.

(1 Sam 16:7)

Knowing what lies ahead for you, you won't become bored with being a Christian, nor become spiritually dull and indifferent.

(Heb 6:12 TLB)

Having predestinated us unto the adoption of children by Jesus Christ to himself, according to the good pleasure of his will.

(Eph 1:5)

Now unto him that is able to do exceeding abundantly above all that we ask or think, according to the power that worketh in us.

(Eph 3:20)

I have an inferiority complex

Our image of ourselves is constructed from the opinions reflected to us by parents, friends and relatives in the early years of our development. A child who feels deeply loved will grow up with a healthy sense of self-worth. A child who is rejected and treated with disrespect will grow up with feelings of deep inferiority. Such a person should be encouraged to view himself through God's eyes. Share with him John 1:42, 'Thou art Simon [Greek: a piece of rock]: thou shalt be Cephas [Greek: a rock].' There were three Simon Peters: (1) the one his friends saw; (2) the one he himself saw; (3) the one Christ saw. Others saw in Peter something small and insignificant (a piece of rock), but Jesus saw in him something strong and secure (a rock). Christ sees us not as we are, but as we can become by his power. Encourage this person to ask himself, 'How does God see me now that I am a Christian?' Help him to answer this by sharing the scriptures listed. You can also challenge him by asking, 'Who is the real you? Is it the person you see yourself? Is it the person your friends see? Or is it the person God sees?' The real self is the person God *means* you to be. Get him to focus on that, to dwell upon it daily in prayer, and the ideal will turn into the actual.

Bible References

For our light affliction, which is but for a moment....
(2 Cor 4:17)

Why art thou cast down, O my soul? ... hope thou in God.

(Ps 42:5)

In God I will praise his word, in God I have put my trust.

(Ps 56:4)

And we know that all things work together for good to them that love God.

(Rom 8:28)

Bow down thine ear to me; deliver me speedily; be thou my strong rock, for an house of defence to save me.
(Ps 31:2)

When thou passeth through the waters, I will be with thee; and through the rivers, they shall not overflow thee.

(Is 43:2)

The Lord is close to those whose hearts are breaking.
(Ps 34:18 TLB)

I am depressed

Bible Reference

Depression should never be viewed lightly. Avoid saying to a depressed person, 'Cheer up,' or, 'Snap out of it.' Such statements are not helpful but, in fact, prove counter-productive. Share with the person some insights from the way God treated Elijah's depression in 1 Kings 19. First, God made sure that Elijah had enough sleep and enough to eat. Lack of sleep and an improper diet are often contributory causes of depression. Second, God waited until Elijah was well rested before he confronted him with the question, 'What doest thou here?' Make sure the person has had enough food and rest before attempting to explore basic causes. Third, God encouraged Elijah to talk about his problem and ventilate his feelings. Be a good listener and encourage the person to share with you what he considers to be the basic cause of his depression. Fourth, God gave Elijah a special task to complete for him. A depressed person needs to become involved in doing something for others, for in this way he breaks the vicious circle of self-centredness which is often a basic cause of his emotional problems. In a case of serious depression, where the person is unable to cope with the ordinary routine duties of life, it is advisable to have a medical check-up. Some forms of depression are chemically based and are greatly helped by proper medication.

Bible References

These trials are only to test your faith, to see whether or not it is strong and pure.

(1 Pet 1:7 TLB)

Everything that has happened to me here has been a great boost in spreading the Good News concerning Christ.

(Phil 1:12 TLB)

The Lord bringeth the counsel of the heathen to nought: he maketh the devices of the people of none effect.

(Ps 33:10)

As far as I am concerned, God turned into good what you meant for evil.

(Gen 50:20 TLB)

Even when we are too weak to have any faith left, he remains faithful to us.

(2 Tim 2:13 TLB)

Take therefore no thought for the morrow: for the morrow shall take thought for the things of itself.

(Mt 6:34)

And now just as you trusted Christ to save you, trust him, too, for each day's problems; live in vital union with him.

(Col 2:6 TLB)

I feel I am a failure

In some way and at some time everyone experiences failure. However, this factor is of little help to someone who may have failed an important examination or a special project. First, work with the person in attempting to discover the cause of the failure. Was it unwise planning, failure to anticipate, attempting something beyond his ability, failing to work hard enough, following wrong advice, etc.? An honest look at the causes will prevent the seeds of failure taking root. Second, allow the person to admit that he has failed. If not honestly faced, it will become repressed and cause further problems at a later stage. Third, encourage him to see the overruling providence of God as illustrated in Romans 8:28. Show that God is not helpless in the face of failure, but can turn everything harmful that happens to us to good. Fourth, if after this advice the person still has deep feelings of failure, then suggest a medical check-up. A Christian doctor says, 'Little by little the human body can become adjusted to feeling below par. Finally you can reach the point where you are really not physically able to handle things the way you should. This can lead to many types of failure in life.'

Bible References

Let not sin therefore reign in your mortal body, that ye should obey it in the lusts thereof.

(Rom 6:12)

For sin shall not have dominion over you; for you are not under the law, but under grace.

(Rom 6:14)

Every man is tempted, when he is drawn away of his own lust, and enticed.

(Jas 1:14)

If any man will come after me, let him deny himself, and take up his cross, and follow me.

(Mt 16:24)

Away then with sinful, earthly things; deaden the evil desires lurking within you; have nothing to do with sexual sin, impurity, lust and shameful desires.

(Col 3:5 TLB)

Don't fool yourselves. Those who live immoral lives— who are idol worshippers, adulterers or homosexuals —will have no share in his kingdom.... There was a time when some of you were just like that, but now your sins are washed away.

(1 Cor 6:9–11 TLB)

I have homosexual tendencies

Homosexual tendencies consist of a sexual attraction for a person of the same sex, and the practice of homosexuality is strongly denounced in the Bible (Lev 20:13; Rom 1:27, 32). Although a homosexual person may feel an inclination towards a person of the same sex, the inclination in itself is not sin. It becomes sin when it is encouraged by fantasizing, or expresses itself in a definite act. Encourage the person to bring about a change in his thought and behaviour patterns through meditation in the Scriptures. Where a definite act of homosexuality has been committed, take the person through the following steps: (1) recognize it as sin; (2) repent of it, asking God's forgiveness; (3) reconstruct the thought-life by meditation in the word of God. Some feel that homosexual tendencies can't be cured. In recent years, however, a growing number of Christians with this problem who have focused on carefully selected passages of Scripture, and meditated upon them, claim that the constant washing of their thoughts by God's word has gradually eliminated their homosexual tendencies. Many of our psychological and spiritual problems stem from wrong thinking. The more a person trains himself to think as God thinks (through Scripture meditation) the greater the possibility of producing right personality development.

Bible References

Be filled with the Spirit.... Wives, submit yourselves unto your own husbands.... Husbands, love your wives....

(Eph 5:18–25)

Be patient with each other, making allowance for each other's faults because of your love.

(Eph 4:2 TLB)

Be humble, thinking of others as better than yourself.

(Phil 2:3 TLB)

Wives, submit yourselves unto your own husbands .... Husbands, love your wives, and be not bitter against them.

(Col 3:18–19)

Give, and it shall be given unto you; good measure, pressed down, and shaken together, and running over.

(Lk 6:38)

You husbands must be careful of your wives, being thoughtful of their needs and honouring them as the weaker sex.

(1 Pet 3:7 TLB)

My marriage is breaking up

There are about twenty to thirty specific reasons why marriages break apart, and many of these can be narrowed down to one basic reason—*self-centredness*. This comes about when one person is more concerned about having his own needs met than in meeting the needs of his partner. In marriage we can be either a *giver* or a *getter*. Givers delight to meet the needs of their partner, while getters are more concerned about having their own needs met. No real progress can be made in dealing with the other problems that arise in marriage unless this is solved. Encourage the person to ask himself this basic question: 'Am I more concerned in meeting the needs of my partner than I am in having my own needs met?' Show him that Christ's love can, if allowed, sweep into his life and shift him from being a self-centred person to a Christ-centred one. Those who are self-centred are 'getters', while Christ-centred people are 'givers'. Use the Scriptures listed to drive this point home. It is important also to point out that the most basic need a man has in his life is the need for *significance*. In a woman the most basic need is *security*. When a man sets out in his marriage to make his wife feel secure, by ministering to her need for security, and the woman in turn focuses on ministering to her husband's need for significance, then in the giving of themselves to each other fulfilment and joy are discovered.

Bible References

Heaviness in the heart of man maketh it stoop: but a good word maketh it glad.

(Prov 12:25)

A sound heart is the life of the flesh; but envy the rottenness of the bones.

(Prov 14:30)

A merry heart doeth good like a medicine.

(Prov 17:22)

Which of you by taking thought can add one cubit unto his stature?

(Mt 6:27)

Be careful for nothing; but in every thing by prayer and supplication... let your requests be made known unto God.

(Phil 4:6–7)

Casting all your care upon him; for he careth for you.
(1 Pet 5:7)

Look at the birds! They don't worry about what to eat... for your heavenly Father feeds them. And you are far more valuable to him than they are.

(Mt 6:26 TLB)

I worry about everything

The basic cause of most worry and anxiety is a failure to handle life on a day-to-day basis. God means us to live our lives one day at a time. Though, of course, it is wise and prudent to plan for the future, we are not to worry about it (Mt 6:31–34). This person will need to be taken to Romans 8:28 and shown that God is in control of all situations, and when human plans are crossed and thwarted, God is able to turn every stumbling block into a stepping-stone. Encourage the person to put all his energy into living a day at a time, as using energy to try to cope with what *might* happen tomorrow is self-defeating. Use the three simple steps below to help him see things in perspective. (1) *What is my problem?* Get him to write this down on a sheet of paper. (2) *What does God want me to do about this problem?* Help him to identify clearly what steps God expects him to take in relation to the problem. Pray with him at this stage. (3) *When, where, and how should I begin?* Plan a simple course of action and encourage him to believe that when he does the *possible* God will do the *impossible*. Someone asked a Negro, a radiant Christian, how he managed to keep free from worry. He replied, 'I know that God won't let anything come my way that he and I together can't handle.' Share this simple but telling truth with the person concerned as well. It has helped thousands of others—it may help again now.

Bible References

Cast thy burden upon the Lord, and he shall sustain thee.

(Ps 55:22)

Let not your heart be troubled: ye believe in God, believe also in me.

(Jn 14:1)

He will swallow up death in victory; and the Lord God will wipe away tears from off all faces.

(Is 25:8)

He will be very gracious unto thee at the voice of thy cry.

(Is 30:19)

O death, where is thy sting? O grave, where is thy victory?

(1 Cor 15:55)

Blessed are they that mourn: for they shall be comforted.

(Mt 5:4)

Blessed is the Lord, for he has shown me that his never-failing love protects me like the walls of a fort!

(Ps 31:21 TLB)

I have lost a loved one

Even when death comes to a loved one after a long illness, grief is still a hard burden to bear. Encourage the bereaved person to talk, as he needs to talk out his inner feelings more than to hear comments or advice. Overcome any tendency he might have to remain silent by gently and lovingly probing him with questions. At an appropriate moment (and if the deceased was a Christian) explain that the Bible pictures death as a great gain for the believer. Share some of the reasons why a Christian is happy in heaven (Rev 21:3–4). If the deceased was not a Christian, discuss some of the positive qualities which he or she possessed. This is being supportive, without going further than God's word and suggesting that there is hope when there is none. Pray with the person concerned and attempt to verbalize his feelings, bringing out into the open buried thoughts and feelings, such as 'Why did this happen?' and 'How can I bear such a loss?' Offer help in a practical way as grief temporarily paralyses routine activities. Be alert for things needing immediate attention. Always offer comfort with sincerity and honesty. If you do not really understand the person's problem, admit it. The most important thing is to let him know that you *care*.

Bible References

Learn to put aside your own desires.... This will make possible the next step, which is for you to enjoy other people and to like them, and finally you will grow to love them deeply.

(2 Pet 1:6–7 TLB)

When a man's ways please the Lord, he maketh even his enemies to be at peace with him.

(Prov 16:7)

Love forgets mistakes; nagging about them parts the best of friends.

(Prov 17:9 TLB)

For the Holy Spirit, God's gift, does not want you to be afraid of people, but to be wise and strong, and to love them and enjoy being with them.

(2 Tim 1:7 TLB)

Now you can have real love for everyone because your souls have been cleansed from selfishness and hatred when you trusted Christ to save you

(1 Pet 1:22 TLB)

A true friend is always loyal, and a brother is born to help in times of need.

(Prov 17:17 TLB)

I have difficulty in making friends

The main reason why people have difficulty in making friends is due to the fact that they have never truly accepted themselves. If we do not accept ourselves, we will have trouble in accepting others, and this negative attitude will be reflected in our relationships. Encourage the person to see himself as God sees him, *in Christ,* a person of immense significance and worth. Tell him 'There never was and never will be another you. You are unique in all the universe.' Once a person discovers his true identity in Christ, his ability to relate to others is greatly improved, as he no longer compares himself to other people but to Christ. Share with him the importance of looking at everyone he meets through Christ's eyes, asking himself two basic questions: 'What is God doing in this person's life?' and 'How can I co-operate with Him?' This attitude will change the focus from 'How can I *get* a friend?' to 'How can I *be* a friend?' As someone once said, 'To have a friend—be friendly.' Share also the five important principles of building friendships. (1) Be alert to each new person around you. (2) Develop a cheerful countenance. (3) Learn people's names, and greet them by name. (4) Ask appropriate questions. (5) Be a good listener.

Bible References

If my people, which are called by my name, shall humble themselves, and pray....

(2 Chron 7:14)

I exhort therefore, that...supplications, prayers, intercessions...be made for all men.

(1 Tim 2:1)

Pray without ceasing. In every thing give thanks.

(1 Thess 5:17–18)

In every thing by prayer and supplication with thanksgiving let your requests be made known unto God.

(Phil 4:6)

When thou prayest, enter into thy closet, and...pray to thy Father.

(Mt 6:6)

For the Lord is watching his children, listening to their prayers.

(1 Pet 3:12 TLB)

Ask, and it shall be given you; seek, and ye shall find; knock, and it shall be opened unto you.

(Lk 11:9)

I find it hard to pray

Offer this person the following suggestions and encourage him to put them into operation immediately. (1) *Make a daily prayer appointment with God and keep it*. In earthly affairs when we make an appointment with someone, we keep that appointment whether we feel like it or not. Making a daily appointment with God means that courtesy will carry us into his presence even if feeling doesn't. (2) *Begin your prayer time by meditating in the Scriptures*. Experience has shown that the best way to begin one's daily prayer is by meditating on a passage from the Bible. This devotional meditation prepares the soul in a wonderful way for fellowship and communion with the Lord. (3) *Use a prayer list*. Put down on a piece of paper items about which you want to pray, and talk to God about them. (4) *Pray out loud, if possible*. Hearing ourselves pray often gives a deeper intensity to prayer. (5) *Don't fight wandering thoughts—use them*. Encourage the person to pray for the thing to which his mind wanders. In this way he can weave even wandering thoughts into the pattern of his prayers. (6) *Thank God for what he has done for you*. God wants us to be thankful. Think on all he has done, and the heart will soon begin to swell with gratitude.

Bible References

Therefore being justified by faith, we have peace with God.

(Rom 5:1)

But as many as received him, to them gave he power to become the sons of God.

(Jn 1:12)

The Spirit itself beareth witness with our spirit, that we are the children of God.

(Rom 8:16)

We know that we have passed from death unto life, because we love the brethren.

(1 Jn 3:14)

If any man be in Christ, he is a new creature.

(2 Cor 5:17)

God is not a man, that he should lie.

(Num 23:19)

Ye have received the Spirit of adoption, whereby we cry, Abba, Father.

(Rom 8:15)

I have doubts about my salvation

A person who has this problem needs to be encouraged to share his understanding of what 'salvation' really means. He may never have understood what it means to be 'saved' and might require the way of salvation explained to him in a clear manner. If, however, he has a clear grasp of its meaning, and has apparently received Christ but lacks assurance, then proceed by asking him the following questions. (1) *When you accepted Christ, did you allow him to take up the centre of your life, or did you relegate him to a marginal part of your being?* Christ is not able to give assurance unless he has been admitted to the central part of one's life. He must be *Lord* as well as Saviour. (2) *When you decided for Christ, did you repent of your sin, or were you just sorry for the consequences?* Some people attempt to become Christians without showing sorrow for the fact they have kept God out of their spirits (the part he made for himself). (3) *Are you holding feelings of bitterness against anyone who has wronged you?* This is often a cause for lack of assurance, as the person is unable to feel the full effect of God's forgiveness until he releases any unforgiveness he holds in his heart towards another.

Bible References

The blood of Jesus Christ... cleanseth us from all sin.

(1 Jn 1:7)

If we confess our sins, he is faithful and just to forgive us our sins.

(1 Jn 1:9)

Let the wicked forsake his way... and let him return unto the Lord, and he will have mercy upon him.

(Is 55:7)

In whom we have... the forgiveness of sins, according to the riches of his grace.

(Eph 1:7)

For thou, Lord, art good, and ready to forgive; and plenteous in mercy.

(Ps 86:5)

It was through what his Son did that God cleared a path for everything to come to him... for Christ's death on the cross has made peace with God for all by his blood.

(Col 1:20 TLB)

Brothers, listen! In this man, Jesus, there is forgiveness for your sins. Everyone who trusts in him is freed from all guilt and declared righteous.

(Acts 13:38–39 TLB)

I have committed a terrible sin

Begin by reading 1 John 1:5 – 2:2 and explain that, providing we take the right steps concerning our sin and adopt the right attitude towards it, then there is no sin that cannot be forgiven. This does not mean that God delights in our sin. He is hurt—deeply hurt—when we violate his laws, but, so great is his love, that he has provided in the shed blood of the Lord Jesus Christ a way by which our sin can be covered and forgiven. Share with the person the following steps. (1) *Confession*. Encourage a full confession in which nothing is held back. Get him to identify the sin by naming it so that he can see it as it really is. (2) *Repentance*. Repentance is not simply being sorry for sin, but being sorry for the deep self-centred attitude that led to it being committed. It is this that must be repented of. (3) *Ask God to forgive, and at the same time receive his forgiveness*. Encourage the person not only to ask but also to accept the forgiveness of God by saying, 'I receive your forgiveness through Jesus Christ, my Lord.' (4) *Take a fresh grip upon God*. Help the person to rededicate himself to God and to his service. (5) *Make restitution if necessary*. If the sin has harmed anyone else, then encourage the person to ask forgiveness of the one who has been hurt, and to put right (as far as is humanly possible) any wrong that has been done.

Bible References

It is his glory to pass over a transgression.

(Prov 19:11)

Forbearing one another, and forgiving one another.

(Col 3:13)

Recompense to no man evil for evil.

(Rom 12:17)

Be ye kind one to another, tenderhearted, forgiving one another.

(Eph 4:32)

If thy brother trespass against thee, rebuke him; and if he repent, forgive him.

(Lk 17:3)

See that none render evil for evil unto any man, but ever follow that which is good.

(1 Thess 5:15)

Your heavenly Father will forgive you if you forgive those who sin against you; but if you refuse to forgive them, he will not forgive you.

(Mt 6:14–15 TLB)

I find it difficult to forgive

The desire to hold bitterness and resentment against someone who has injured us lies deep in the human heart. Unforgiveness, however, has serious spiritual and psychological consequences. Explain to the person concerned that forgiveness involves two things: (1) wiping the slate clean in relation to the offence; and (2) handing over to God the responsibility for discipline or punishment. It is important to make this clear, as some people say they are willing to forgive but not to forget. Next, get the person to make a list of the hurts and offences which need to be forgiven. This ensures that nothing remains hidden to come up at another time. Then encourage the person to view these hurts and offences from God's point of view. Show him that God has been using hurts to improve his character, as the offences and injuries suffered by us become, in God's hands, the best 'teachers' for developing our characters and spiritual effectiveness. Next, get him to reflect on what God has done for him: as we see the depth of God's forgiveness in our lives, it motivates us towards the forgiveness of others. Finally, show him that forgiveness is an act of the will. If we wait until we feel like forgiving, we may never do it. We must obey the command of Ephesians 4:32 and say, by an act of the will, 'I forgive this person in Jesus' name, just as Christ has forgiven me.'

Bible References

This poor man cried, and the Lord heard him, and saved him out of all his troubles.

(Ps 34:6)

We are perplexed because we don't know why things happen as they do, but we don't give up.... We get knocked down, but we get up again and keep going.

(2 Cor 4:8–9 TLB)

God... will not allow you to be tested beyond your power to remain firm; at the time you are put to the test, he will give you the strength to endure it, and so provide you with a way out.

(1 Cor 10:13 GNB)

Let us therefore come boldly unto the throne of grace, that we may obtain mercy, and find grace to help in time of need.

(Heb 4:16)

Even when we are too weak to have any faith left, he remains faithful to us and will help us, for he cannot disown us who are part of himself.

(2 Tim 2:13 TLB)

I intend to commit suicide

When confronted by this statement, the first thing you should do is to *communicate your personal interest* by letting the person know how glad you are that he shared this information with you. Be a good listener and encourage him to talk over the problem with you. Be sure not to challenge or criticize anything he says, or make any value judgements on his behaviour at this stage. Try to clarify the basic problem as quickly as possible. Say something like this: 'I'm interested in knowing what it is that has brought you to these conclusions. Would you like to share them with me?' Concentrate on piecing together the bits of information you receive from the distressed person, in order to put the whole problem into perspective. When you have clarified what the problem is, then share with the person concerned a sense of hope that you will personally assist in helping him solve the problem. The cardinal rules of helping those who are suicidal are these: (1) *Activity*—the person needs to feel something is being done; (2) *Authority*—the person needs to feel that you are able to take charge; (3) *Involvement*—the person needs to feel that you will take a personal interest in the solution of his problem.

Please turn to the next page for further instructions on how to handle suicidal cases.

Dos and don'ts

IN RELATION TO THE SUICIDAL

DO take seriously every suicidal threat, comment, or act. Suicide is no joke. Don't be afraid to ask the person if he is really thinking about committing suicide. The mention won't plant the idea in his head. Rather, it will relieve him to know that he is being taken seriously, that he is better understood than he suspected.

DON'T dismiss a suicidal threat or underestimate its importance. Never say, 'Forget it. You won't kill yourself. You can't really mean it. You're not the type.' That kind of remark may be a challenge to a suicidal person. Such a person needs attention, not dismissal. Anyone desperate enough can be 'the type'.

DON'T try to shock or challenge the person by saying, 'Go ahead and do it.' Such an impatient remark may be hard to hold back if a person has been repeating his threats or has been bothersome to have around. But it is a careless invitation to suicide.

DON'T try to analyse the person's behaviour and confront him with interpretations of his actions and feelings during the moment of crisis. That should be done later by a professional.

DON'T argue with the individual about whether he should live or die. That argument can't be won. The only possible position to take is that the person *must* live.

DON'T assume that time heals all wounds and everything will get better by itself. That can happen, but it can't be counted on.

DO be willing to listen. You may have heard the story before, but hear it again. Be genuinely interested, be strong, stable and firm. Promise the person that everything possible will be done to keep him alive, because that is what he needs most.

Published by the Public Affairs Committee in New York.

Section B

The winning of a soul to Jesus Christ is the greatest joy known to man. Unfortunately, comparatively few Christians are equipped to deal with earnest enquirers, and fewer still are able to answer the honest doubts of a seeking soul.

The following section deals with twelve problems often raised by the unconverted, and contains also some helpful suggestions and Scripture references to use when dealing with these problems.

These suggestions are not given so that you can demonstrate to the unconverted your intellectual or spiritual superiority. No one is won into the kingdom of God by being beaten in an argument. Be loving, persuasive, and share the truth with a genuine concern for the other person's spiritual well-being.

'If anybody asks why you believe as you do, be ready to tell him, and do it in a gentle and respectful way' (1 Pet 3:15 TLB).

Difficulties
of the unconverted

Bible References

Though your sins be as scarlet, they shall be as white as snow.

(Is 1:18)

The Son of Man is come to seek and to save....

(Lk 19:10)

I am not come to call the righteous, but sinners.

(Mt 9:13)

Christ Jesus came into the world to save sinners; of whom I am chief.

(1 Tim 1:15)

For whosoever shall call upon the name of the Lord shall be saved.

(Rom 10:13)

Whosoever believeth in him shall receive remission of sins.

(Acts 10:43)

Behold the Lamb of God, which taketh away the sin of the world.

(Jn 1:29)

I am too great a sinner

When attempting to help anyone who has made this, or a similar statement, never give the impression that their sins are *not* great. Sin is an offence to God and should never be minimized. Say something like this: 'There can be no doubt that God looks upon sin as something repulsive to his holy nature, but because he loves each one of us with an unconditional love he has thought up a way by which sin, however bad and evil it is, can be forgiven.' Open your Bible at Isaiah 53:6 and invite the person you are dealing with to read the verse out loud. Then ask the question: 'What does this verse say God has done with sin?' The answer of course is quite plain—he has laid it upon Christ. If the person is slow in seeing this truth, or hesitant to respond, use the following illustration. Take a book (or any other object) in your hand and say, 'Let this book represent your sin, my left hand represent you, and my right hand represent Christ.' Place the book (or object) on your left hand and ask the person, 'Where is your sin now?' Encourage them to answer, 'On me.' Then place the book on your right hand (the hand which represents Christ) and ask, 'Where is your sin now?' The answer of course is that the sin is on Christ. Follow up this illustration by pointing the person to some of the Scriptures opposite which show that Christ has paid the penalty for *every* human sin. John 1:29 and Acts 10:43 are particularly helpful here. Another helpful insight to use is to show the person that although he considers himself to be a great sinner, he cannot claim to be the *greatest* sinner. Paul claimed that in 1 Timothy 1:15. And if the *greatest* sinner has been saved then salvation is possible to every other human being.

Bible References

Seek ye first the kingdom of God....

(Mt 6:33)

Behold, now is the accepted time; behold now is the day of salvation.

(2 Cor 6:2)

But God said... Thou fool, this night thy soul shall be required of thee.

(Lk 12:20)

Walk while ye have the light, lest darkness come upon you.

(Jn 12:35)

Whereas ye know not what shall be on the morrow.

(Jas 4:14)

Strive to enter in at the strait gate; for many... will seek to enter in, and shall not be able.

(Lk 13:24)

Seek ye the Lord while he may be found, call ye upon him while he is near.

(Is 55:6)

He, that... hardeneth his neck, shall suddenly be destroyed.

(Prov 29:1)

I'll decide one day
— but not today

A good verse to use with someone who adopts this position is Isaiah 55:6. Invite the person to read the verse aloud and then pose the question: '*When* are you to seek the Lord?' After the answer is given, 'While he may be found,' ask *when* that is. The person will usually be perplexed at this point, but use the moment to show that no one has any guarantee that Christ can be found tomorrow. Death, natural disasters, or the possibility of an accident make life most uncertain. Ask the person this question: 'Can you be sure of finding Christ tomorrow if you do not seek him today?' Another useful verse to use, when dealing with a person's tendency to procrastinate, is Proverbs 29:1. Once again get the person to read the verse aloud, and then ask the question: 'What becomes of the one who "being often reproved hardeneth his neck"?' When the answer is given, 'He shall be destroyed,' follow with another question—'How?' When the person answers with the word 'suddenly', bear down on this point and encourage the person not to take unnecessary risks with the important issue of eternal salvation. Dr Chalmers, a famous evangelist, used to use the following method when dealing with procrastinators. He would say, 'Would you be prepared to wait a year and have no opportunity, under any circumstances, no matter what came up, of accepting Christ?' When the person answered, 'No, I might die within a year,' Dr Chalmers would then say, 'Well, would you be willing to wait a month?' Gradually he would bring it down to a week, and then a day, saying, 'Would you like God and the Holy Spirit to leave you alone for a day and not have an opportunity under any circumstances of accepting Christ?' The great man won many people to Christ following this method. And so can you.

Bible References

Who are kept by the power of God through faith unto salvation.

(1 Pet 1:5)

To him who is able to keep you from falling....

(Jude 24)

Christ liveth in me.

(Gal 2:20)

He is able to keep....

(2 Tim 1:12)

My sheep...follow me...and I give unto them eternal life.

(Jn 10:27–28)

God is able to make him stand....

(Rom 14:4)

But the Lord is faithful, who shall establish you.

(2 Thess 3:3)

God...will not suffer you to be tempted above that ye are able.

(1 Cor 10:13)

I'll never be able to keep it up

Point out to the person who presents this problem that the Christian life, when lived out under one's own personal strength and effort, is not just difficult—it's impossible. There is no way a person can live a truly Christian life in his own strength. Christ has to live his life in and through that person, or else the whole thing falls to pieces. Illustrate the point by taking a pencil in your right hand and then placing it vertically on your left palm. Then take your hand away. The pencil of course no longer supported by your right hand will fall over. Do this several times, and then press home the point that only Christ is able to uphold us and 'keep us from falling' (Jude 24). Explain that when a person becomes a Christian, he receives from Christ a new nature and a special supply of God's power, which enables him to live the Christian life in the strength of Christ himself. Go on to say that the Christian religion is the only religion in the world whose founder came back from the dead to live his life in the personalities of his followers. John 10:28–29 beautifully shows that the safety of the person who accepts Christ does not depend on that person's ability to 'hold out' but upon the keeping power of the Father and the Son. 2 Timothy 1:12 shows also that it is Christ's business and not ours to keep that which is entrusted to him, and that he is well able to do it. Jude 24 points out that whether we can keep from falling or not, Christ is able to support us. 1 Corinthians 10:13 is especially useful to show a person who is afraid that some strong temptation will overcome him and he will fall. Emphasize to the person that 'the Christian life is not your responsibility, but your response to his ability'.

Bible References

There is none righteous, no, not one.

(Rom 3:10)

All we like sheep have gone astray.

(Is 53:6)

For as many as are of the works of the law are under the curse.

(Gal 3:10)

But as many as received him, to them gave he power to become the sons of God.

(Jn 1:12)

If thou shalt confess with thy mouth the Lord Jesus, and shalt believe in thine heart that God hath raised him from the dead, thou shalt be saved.

(Rom 10:9)

Except ye be converted, and become as little children, you shall not enter into the kingdom of heaven.

(Mt 18:3)

I've always believed in Jesus

This is regarded as the most common objection and difficulty found in people who have not experienced a genuine conversion. A person who makes this statement is really entertaining a false hope. He (or she) thinks that by merely believing in Jesus as an historical figure, salvation is automatically ensured. Take the person through the basic steps of salvation and show them that in order to be saved and have a guaranteed place in heaven one must have a *personal* encounter with Jesus Christ. This means knowing him as distinct from knowing about him. Explain these simple steps: (1) because of Adam and Eve's original transgression in the garden of Eden every man and woman is born into this world a sinner (Is 53:6; Rom 3:23); (2) as God cannot allow sin in heaven, he provided a way whereby sin could be forgiven through the death of his own Son on the cross (Rom 5:6, 8); (3) in order fully to experience forgiveness for sin, everyone must personally receive the benefit of Christ's death on the cross. It is not enough that Christ has died; to be saved one must appropriate the benefits of his death by personally repenting of sin and receiving Christ into one's life as Lord and Saviour (Rom 10:9; Acts 3:19). You will need to make clear to this person the difference between head belief and heart belief. For example, a person may believe a plane can carry him safely across the Atlantic, yet for some reason he may be unwilling to commit himself to travelling on it. His belief therefore is merely in his head. Only when he settles down in the aircraft—commits himself to it—is he really demonstrating his belief. Faith is like that: no one can truly experience Christ's provision of salvation until he is willing to commit himself to it—fully and completely.

Bible References

The Lord is ... not willing that any should perish.
(2 Pet 3:9)

And ye will not come to me, that ye might have life.
(Jn 5:40)

As I live, saith the Lord God, I have no pleasure in the death of the wicked ... Why will ye die?
(Ezek 33:11)

He that believeth not the Son shall not see life.
(Jn 3:36)

Except ye repent, ye shall all likewise perish.
(Lk 13:3)

If ye believe not ... ye shall die in your sins.
(Jn 8:24)

God is too good to damn anyone

This person needs to be shown that the same Bible which tells of God's goodness also points out another ingredient in his character—justice. To be just God has to punish sin. God does not send anyone to hell—it is sin that does that. The Scriptures opposite show that it is not so much God who damns men and women as them damning themselves by rejecting God's offer of mercy and forgiveness as expressed through the cross. A person does not go to hell because he is bad, neither does he go to heaven because he is good. He goes to either of the two places *according to his relationship with Jesus Christ*. Explain that God's goodness is seen in the way he provides us with salvation from the consequences of our sin (which is hell). Read Romans 2:4–5 to the person and say something like this: 'Now you can see from what God says here that the purpose of his goodness is to lead you to repentance, not to encourage you to sin, and when you trample on his goodness you are building up a terrible punishment for yourself.' John 8:21, 24 and John 3:16 show clearly that, however good God may be, he will most certainly reject those who reject his Son. You can also say, 'You see, God is not willing that anyone should perish, and he offers the gift of eternal life to you, but there is one difficulty in the way. Would you like to know what it is?' When the person replies, refer him to John 5:40 to see what the difficulty is. The passage reads, 'Ye will not come to me, that ye might have life.' You can conclude by saying lovingly and compassionately, 'In Christ God offers you forgiveness for your sin and the gift of eternal life. If you won't accept it, then God has no other alternative but to allow you to perish.'

Bible References

Thou art inexcusable...whosoever thou art that judgest.

(Rom 2:1)

First cast out the beam out of thine own eye.

(Mt 7:5)

Thus saith the Lord, what iniquity have your fathers found in me?

(Jer 2:5)

If ye forgive not men their trespasses, neither will your Father forgive your trespasses.

(Mt 6:15)

Forgiving one another, even as God for Christ's sake hath forgiven you.

(Eph 4:32)

Peter...said, Lord, how oft shall my brother sin against me, and I forgive him? till seven times? Jesus saith... Until seventy times seven.

(Mt 18:21–22)

There are too many hypocrites in the church

This argument is usually advanced by those who, in some way, have been mistreated by a professing Christian. Encourage the person to talk about this, as ventilating the problem will make it easier for him to receive what you have to say. Using Romans 14:4 and 12, show him that he is solely responsible for his own relationship with God, and what others do bears little relation to the issue. Endeavour to turn the person's attention from how others have treated him to see how God has treated him. Jeremiah 2:5, Isaiah 53:5 and Romans 5:6-8 are useful for this purpose. Ask the person if, even though a Christian has treated him badly, this is any excuse for his treatment of a heavenly Father who has treated him with such tenderness and concern. An evangelist who asked a man if he was a Christian received this reply: 'No I am not. And the reason I am not a Christian is because other Christians have treated me badly.' The evangelist turned to his Bible and read Jeremiah 2:5—'Thus saith the Lord, What iniquity have your fathers found in me, that they have gone far from me, and have walked after vanity, and are become vain?' He then said, 'Did you find any iniquity in God? Has not God treated you well?' The man admitted that the Almighty had not treated him badly and responded to the evangelist's invitation to receive Christ into his life. Point out also that it is only when we are prepared to forgive others who have hurt us that we can fully experience God's forgiveness. Matthew 6:17–15; 18:23–35 and Ephesians 4:30–32 are useful Scriptures to use when attempting to do this.

Bible References

God took the sinless Christ and poured into him our sins. Then, in exchange, he poured God's goodness into us!

(2 Cor 5:21 TLB)

Repent...for the kingdom of heaven is at hand.

(Mt 3:2)

God...commandeth all men every where to repent.

(Acts 17:30)

Every tongue should confess that Jesus Christ is Lord.

(Phil 2:11)

The goodness of God leadeth thee to repentance.

(Rom 2:4)

Repent, and be baptized every one of you in the name of Jesus Christ.

(Acts 2:38)

Except ye repent, ye shall all likewise perish.

(Luke 13:3)

I've tried before but failed

When a person makes this statement it usually means that they previously failed to experience a true conversion. A true conversion takes place when a person *repents of sin*. Every counsellor must have a clear concept of what sin is, and what repentance is, as lacking this insight any attempt to help a person will prove unproductive. What is sin? The Bible defines sin as something more than wrongdoing. It is allowing life to revolve around ourselves instead of God. Sin is anarchy in the human spirit, challenging the very right of God to rule. Sin rules therefore by keeping self instead of God in the centre of our lives. And what is repentance? Repentance is more than being sorry for our wrongdoing. It goes down to the roots of our being and recognizes that God has been excluded from the part of the personality which he made for himself—the spirit. A person can be sorry about their sins and think by doing so they have repented. This is not repentance; this is regret. Repentance is recognizing that inside of us there is a basic self-centredness that wants its own way, then firmly removing this self-centredness by allowing Jesus Christ to come into the spirit (the part he made for himself) as Saviour and Lord. People who invite Christ into a marginal part of their lives and never give him the centre (the spirit) cannot experience a true conversion, because the self still rules at the centre. Ask the person 'When you invited Christ into your life, did you surrender your self-centredness and allow Christ to be Lord?' Sin is really saying to God, 'I want to run my life on my own terms.' Repentance is saying to God, 'Lord, you take over and run my life the way you want it run.' Ponder these insights until they are clear to you. Without them you will not be able to help a person experience a genuine conversion.

Bible References

In thy presence is fulness of joy.

(Ps 16:11)

He that spared not his own Son... how shall he not... give us all things?

(Rom 8:32)

What shall it profit a man, if he shall gain the whole world, and lose his own soul?

(Mk 8:36)

I count all things but loss for the excellency of the knowledge of Christ.

(Phil 3:8)

No good thing will he withhold from them that walk uprightly.

(Ps 84:11)

The thief cometh... to steal, and to kill, and to destroy: I am come that they might have life, and that they might have it more abundantly.

(Jn 10:10)

I have too much to give up

Mark 8:34–38 is extremely useful to share with a person who has this problem. After reading it to the person, or getting the person to read it himself—out loud—point out that in relation to the matter of your eternal destiny it is better by far to give up everything you possess than to lose your soul. Follow this by referring the person to Philippians 3:7–8, which shows that whatever a person gives up for Christ is nothing compared to what they receive from him. Psalm 84:11 and Romans 8:32 show also that God will never ask anyone to give up anything that is helpful to their lives—only the harmful. An experienced evangelist, who was confronted by a young woman with this objection, asked her, 'Do you believe that God loves you?' 'Yes,' she said, 'I believe that.' 'How much do you think he loves you?' She pondered the question for a little while, and said, 'I suppose he loved me enough to give his Son to die for me on the cross.' 'Now,' said the evangelist, 'do you really think that, if God loved you enough to give his only Son to die for you, he will ask you to give up anything that is not for your good?' The girl saw the point and surrendered her life to Christ that very moment. You see, at the heart of this problem lies a wrong concept of God. The person sees God as someone who wants to take away rather than someone who wants to give. It is part of your counselling to change the person's perspective by focusing on those scriptures that show God to be a generous and magnanimous giver. 'Jesus Christ,' said one famous evangelist, 'is not a thief. He isn't in the business of robbing people of their pleasure. He is more concerned about giving than getting, enriching rather than depleting, adding to a person's life—not taking away.'

Bible References

Man shall not live by bread alone, but by every word that proceedeth out of the mouth of God.

(Mt 4:4)

For the word of God is quick, and powerful, and sharper than any two-edged sword.

(Heb 4:12)

If any of you really determines to do God's will, then he will certainly know whether my teaching is from God or is merely my own.

(Jn 7:17 TLB)

But the natural man receiveth not the things of the Spirit of God ... because they are spiritually discerned.

(1 Cor 2:14)

The secret of the Lord is with them that fear him.

(Ps 25:14)

All scripture is given by inspiration of God.

(2 Tim 3:16)

The god of this world hath blinded the minds of them which believe not.

(2 Cor 4:4)

I don't believe the Bible

Those who use this argument think that having dismissed the Bible they can frustrate any attempt on your part to win them to Christ. Although there are times when an intellectual approach is necessary to rebut arguments concerning the word of God, don't depend too much on intellectual argument. Use the word of God freely and fearlessly—then watch it work! One approach you can use is to suggest to the person that he or she would hardly dismiss the world's most important piece of literature without knowing something of its main theme and message—ask them to summarize its main theme for you. Most people will say 'The Golden Rule' or 'The Ten Commandments'. You can then point out gently and tactfully that the main theme of the Bible is to show us how to have eternal life. You can then turn the tables and say something like this: 'Let me share with you, if I may, what the Bible's main message is.' Then proceed to outline the way of salvation. Use biblical passages freely, as there is tremendous power in repeating the word of God to the unconverted. Romans 3:3–4 is extremely useful to show that questioning a fact does not alter a fact. 2 John 10 is a powerful verse to use and shows that a person who does not believe or live by the doctrine of Christ is lost. Remember, however, when using texts such as these, which are strongly confronting, not to use them as battering rams to break open a person's heart. Your purpose should not be to win an argument, but to win a soul. Actually 2 John 10 has been greatly used by the Holy Spirit to convince sceptics of the reliability and authority of God's word; but it must be presented gently, lovingly and compassionately. It is an awesome responsibility to tell someone he is lost. There should be tears in your voice, if not in your eyes.

Bible References

He that believeth not the Son...the wrath of God abideth on him.

(Jn 3:36)

For the wages of sin is death; but the gift of God is eternal life.

(Rom 6:23)

Whosoever committeth sin is the servant of sin.

(Jn 8:34)

If ye believe not... ye shall die in your sins.

(Jn 8:24)

And whosoever was not found written in the book of life was cast into the lake of fire.

(Rev 20:15)

And this is the condemnation, that light is come into the world, and men loved darkness rather than light.

(Jn 3:19)

He, that being often reproved hardeneth his neck, shall suddenly be destroyed, and that without remedy.

(Prov 29:1)

It is a fearful thing to fall into the hands of the living God.

(Heb 10:31)

I'm just not interested in anything religious

Many people reject the concepts of God, Christ, heaven, hell, etc., because to accept them would produce deep and disturbing feelings within their hearts. Instead of facing these feelings and dealing with them, many people reject the thought of anything religious in the hope that this will dispense with anxious feelings about their spiritual condition. As God has built into every man and woman a conscience and a sensitivity to the laws of God (Jn 1:9) you can activate the conscience by well-placed questions. One question you can ask is this: 'Do you know that you have committed one of the greatest sins a human being can commit on this earth?' When the person asks you to explain, read Matthew 22:37–38 and ask him if he has kept the first and greatest commandment. When he says no, point out that to violate the greatest commandment is to commit the greatest sin. Note, however, that this question ought not to be put arrogantly or jocularly. Be serious as you present it, asking God to help you break through the person's apparent indifference. Often you will meet with someone who is not willing to sit and let you deal with him in the way described above. In that case the only thing you can do is to ask God's guidance in giving the person a short, powerful and pointed verse of Scripture. Many evangelists can testify to the power of such texts as Hebrews 10:31 or Romans 6:23, which given as a passing shot have been used by the Holy Spirit to bring a person to Christ. Once again, it is important to remember not to use these texts in the wrong spirit. Share them wisely, lovingly and compassionately.

Bible References

Him that cometh to me I will in no wise cast out.

(Jn 6:37)

If thou shalt confess...and shalt believe in thine heart...thou shalt be saved.

(Rom 10:9)

Whosoever shall call upon the name of the Lord shall be saved.

(Rom 10:13)

Through his name whosoever believeth in him shall receive remission of sins.

(Acts 10:43)

Come now, and let us reason together...though your sins be as scarlet, they shall be as white as snow.

(Is 1:18)

Come unto me, all ye that labour and are heavy laden, and I will give you rest.

(Mt 11:28)

And I say unto you, Ask, and it shall be given you; seek, and ye shall find; knock, and it shall be opened unto you. For every one that asketh receiveth.

(Lk 11:9–10)

I've committed the unpardonable sin

This is often the most difficult problem to deal with, as in most cases where this statement is made it is presented with a good deal of emotional distress. Anyone who claims to have committed the unpardonable sin is hardly likely to have done so, for if they had, they would have no feeling of personal concern over their soul's salvation and would manifest no desire to be forgiven. A person with this problem usually has deep emotional difficulties stemming from past relationships with parents or peers, bringing about a restriction in spiritual understanding. A person who has gone through negative experiences in childhood, and who was not warmly and lovingly nurtured, will, because of damaged emotions, tend to project their fears, guilts and hurts on to God and imagine him to be as unloving and as uncaring as the people they encountered in their past. Nine times out of ten, therefore, this problem is a psychological one rather than a spiritual one. The word of God is quick and sharp and powerful (Heb 4:12) and can break through all barriers, so use it to bring about spiritual understanding. Explain that the unpardonable sin (Mt 12:22–32) is really a calculated and contrived resistance to God's Holy Spirit, in which the person concerned refuses to believe what deep in his heart he knows to be true. It is not something that happens in a moment, but is a consistent and continued revolt against truth, light and holiness, similar to the rebellion of the angels in heaven and for whom there was no offer of forgiveness or salvation. Use the scriptures listed on the opposite page and keep using them in the face of all argument. A little patient and prayerful counselling will often bring about a solution to this problem.

Bible References

God so loved the world, that he gave his only begotten Son.

(Jn 3:16)

No man is justified by the law in the sight of God.

(Gal 3:11)

Thou shalt love the Lord thy God with all thy heart, and with all thy soul, and with all thy mind.

(Mt 22:37)

Without faith it is impossible to please . . . God.

(Heb 11:6)

He that believeth on the Son hath everlasting life.

(Jn 3:36)

Except your righteousness shall exceed that of the . . . Pharisees, ye shall in no case enter into the kingdom of heaven.

(Mt 5:20)

And the Word was made flesh, and dwelt among us.

(Jn 1:14)

I do my best — isn't that good enough?

Many rest their hope of eternal salvation on this false foundation. The way to undermine this position is to show the person from Matthew 22:36–40 the standard which God has set for all men and women. Ask the person if he has kept this commandment. When he admits to having broken it show him from James 2:10 that having broken one commandment he is as guilty before God as if he had broken them all. Point out also that if doing one's best is all that is necessary to get to heaven, then God made a mistake in sending his Son to this earth to die upon a cross. Use this story to illustrate the point. A Christian, when witnessing one day to a barber, received the reply, 'I am doing my best—surely God will accept that.' The Christian said nothing, but when the barber had finished cutting his hair he rose from the chair and offered to help the barber cut the hair of his waiting customers. 'But you can't do that,' protested the barber, 'you haven't been trained.' 'But I will do my best,' said the Christian. 'Do you think your best will be good enough for my customers?' said the barber. 'No,' replied the Christian, 'and neither is your best good enough for God.' Point out to the person that Christianity is different from every other religion. Other religions try to climb the ladder that leads up to God, but because it is too high and God is so far off they can never make it. Christ shows that God has come down the ladder by means of the Incarnation. The Son of God became the Son of man in order that the sons of men might become the sons of God. He came to do for us what we could not do for ourselves.

Suggestions to adopt

WHEN DEALING WITH THE UNCONVERTED

- Depend on the Holy Spirit, not your argument, to illuminate people's minds.

- Don't be too *intense* in your approach. This puts people off.

- Listen carefully to what the other person has to say.

- Ask yourself: 'Why is this question bothering him?' It will help you uncover the root cause underlying the question.

- Differentiate between the person and the problem. Don't allow any difficulty you may have in convincing the person of Christ's claims to interfere with your respect for him as a person.

- Keep using the Bible as your authority. There is an awesome power in biblical texts when used.

- Don't be afraid to admit when you have no answer. Tell the person you will *find* the answer.

- Keep refocusing the issue on to Jesus Christ. Other issues can become vague but *he* is always clear.

Section C

The last section deals with the intellectual excuses which thinking people often give as reasons for rejecting Christ and the truth of Christianity. It is important to see these for what they are—'excuses', and not genuine problems. Josh McDowell, an evangelist who has been deeply involved in dealing with university and college students, and has ministered in over 400 universities in 42 countries, says, 'I have met many men with intellectual excuses, but few with intellectual problems.'

The truth is that most people (not all) who advance intellectual arguments as to why they reject Christianity, do so, not because they have a genuine intellectual problem, but because they are unprepared and unwilling to submit their wills to Jesus Christ, and have their life-style radically changed.

Generally speaking, there are four basic reasons why people reject Christianity:

1. **Ignorance.** These are the people who have never read the Bible or heard the way of salvation. In many cases this ignorance, however, is self-imposed, as deep in their hearts they are aware of their moral accountability to God, but they keep their distance from anything religious in an attempt to use ignorance as a final excuse for rejecting the God that nature and their conscience tell them exists (Rom 1:18–20).

2. **Pride.** These are the people who struggle to maintain a self-centred position in the midst of their own universe, and will not admit that they need God's help in obtaining eternal salvation (Jn 5:40–44).

3. **Bitterness.** These claim that there is so much suffering and injustice in the world that God cannot

possibly be interested in the affairs of the inhabitants of the earth. 'If he is not concerned with us,' they claim, 'why should we be concerned with him?'

4. **Moral impurity.** These are so caught up in sensuality and the pleasures of the flesh that they are unwilling to give up their present life-style. They resent the fact that God will demand an inward change, and so they choose to reject him.

It is often true that people reject Christ not because of problems in their minds but because of a problem with their will. It is not so much 'I can't' but 'I won't'. A counsellor when discussing an intellectual excuse with a brilliant young university student said, 'If I can prove to your satisfaction the claim of Christianity to be true, will you then receive Christ?' Her reply was no. He said, 'Then your problem is not in your mind, but in your will.' It is important in dealing with non-Christians to point out whenever they refuse to accept the argument for Christianity that their problem might not be intellectual (in the mind) but volitional (in the will).

Paul Little has pointed out that every Christian has a responsibility to try to answer the intellectual arguments of thoughtful and thinking people. He claims that there are two wrong positions that Christians can adopt in relation to this matter:

1. An anti-intellectual attitude in which they withdraw from all discussion at an intellectual level.
2. A pro-intellectual attitude in which they think that all that is necessary is skilful argument and reasoned debate.

John Stott has said that 'while we must not pande
a man's intellectual arrogance, we must cater t

intellectual integrity'. We owe it to thinking men and women to give 'a reason for the hope that is within us'.

On the other hand, we must not overemphasize this and go to the other extreme. People are won to Christ not by human argument (though that helps) but by the regenerating power of the Holy Spirit. There must always be complete and utter dependency on him, for 'no one can say, "Jesus is Lord," and really mean it, unless the Holy Spirit is helping him' (1 Cor 12:3 TLB).

Some years ago a group of Christians working with university students were impressed by the fact that in their discussions with young intellectuals certain questions kept recurring. They discovered that eight basic questions kept coming up time after time in discussion. These eight questions, together with counselling suggestions, form the next section of this booklet. Acquainting yourself with these questions will help you in your task of dealing with those who offer intellectual excuses.

Intellectual excuses

Bible References

And there came a voice out of the cloud, saying, This is my beloved Son: hear him.

(Lk 9:35)

And the Word was made flesh, and dwelt among us... full of... truth.

(Jn 1:14)

Truth came by Jesus Christ.

(Jn 1:17)

The true worshippers shall worship the Father in spirit and in truth: for the Father seeketh such.

(Jn 4:23)

Then said Jesus to those... which believed on him... Ye shall know the truth, and the truth shall make you free.

(Jn 8:31–32)

Jesus said... no man cometh unto the Father, but by me.

(Jn 14:6)

Neither is there salvation in any other: for there is none other name under heaven given among men, whereby we must be saved.

(Acts 4:12)

Aren't all religions just different paths to the same God?

The inference behind this question is that adherents of other religions worship the same God as a Christian, only under a different name; so why should Christians insist that Jesus is the only way to God? The most important thing in life is truth. It has been said: 'Faith is no more valid than the object in which it is placed.' If we want to get to heaven, then we owe it to ourselves to make sure that our faith is pinned on that which is true. As non-Christian religions differ from the Christian religion over the place given to Jesus Christ, and as Christ himself said that he is the only way to God, then the matter is crucial. Whom are we to believe? Christ himself or those who have framed the world's religions? There may be many paths by which we come to Jesus Christ, but Jesus Christ himself said that *he* is the only way by which we come to God. Do not be afraid of being regarded as bigoted when presenting the truth of the pre-eminence and indispensability of Christ. The issue is too critical, as there is no other option apart from Christ. If you are going to be faithful to what Christ says, then take your stand firmly and positively on the truth of the Scripture that there is but one way to God and that way is through the Person of God's Son, Jesus Christ himself.

Bible References

God said unto Moses...say...I AM hath sent me unto you.

(Ex 3:14)

Jesus said...I AM the bread of life...the living bread which came down from heaven.

(Jn 6:35, 51)

Jesus saith...I AM the way, the truth, and the life.
(Jn 14:6)

In the beginning was the Word, and the Word was with God, and the Word was God....All things were made by him....And the Word was made flesh, and dwelt among us.

(Jn 1:1, 3, 14)

I and my Father are one.

(Jn 10:30)

He that hath seen me hath seen the Father.

(Jn 14:9)

But unto the Son he saith, Thy throne, O God, is for ever and ever; a sceptre of righteousness is the sceptre of thy kingdom.

(Heb 1:8)

Is Jesus Christ really God?

Someone has said that the 'acid test of Christianity is Christ'. In other words, Christianity rises and falls on the position we give to Jesus Christ. If Jesus Christ is not God, then he cannot possibly give salvation to men. The following scriptural arguments will help you disprove the theory that Jesus Christ is not God. (1) If Christ is not God, then he was wrong to accept the worship of Thomas (Jn 20:28), for worship given to a creature or a created being is idolatry. (2) If Jesus Christ is not God, then how is it that his most intimate friends came to believe and teach that he was? (3) If Jesus Christ is not God, then why does the Scripture give him equal status with God in the creation of the universe? (Compare Gen 1:1 and Col 1:16.) (4) If Jesus Christ is not God, then how can he claim to forgive sins, seeing this right belongs to God alone (Mt 9:6)? (5) If Jesus Christ is not God, then why did he teach that all men should honour him just as they should honour the Father (Jn 5:22–23)? In this passage it can be seen that Jesus presents a warning to those who accuse him of blasphemy. He tells them that by hurling abuse at him they are actually hurling it at God, and God is offended by their treatment of his Son. It is quite clear from this that to dishonour Jesus is to dishonour God, for Jesus *is* God.

Bible References

They that be whole need not a physician, but they that are sick…for I am not come to call the righteous, but sinners to repentance.

(Mt 9:12–13)

Wherefore I say unto thee, Her sins, which are many, are forgiven; for she loved much: but to whom little is forgiven, the same loveth little.

(Lk 7:47)

Not many wise men…not many mighty, not many noble, are called: but God hath chosen the foolish…the weak…and base…and things which are not…that no flesh should glory in his presence.

(1 Cor 1:26–29)

If any man be in Christ, he is a new creature: old things are passed away; behold, all things are become new.

(2 Cor 5:17)

By the grace of God I am what I am.

(1 Cor 15:10)

'I don't know whether he is good or bad,' the man replied, 'but I know this: I was blind, and now I see!'

(Jn 9:25 TLB)

Can't Christianity be explained psychologically?

The inference behind this question is that Christians are the product of childhood conditioning and psychological pressures. The thought is sometimes advanced that people become Christians because of what they were taught in their childhood days, and by so doing respond to preconditioning. This is an over-simplification of the issue, as a good deal of evidence can be advanced to show that Christians come from every imaginable background, many being converted to Christ from an atheistic upbringing or an agnostic family. Another inference in this argument is that Christians become changed individuals through self-hypnosis—they hypnotize themselves into believing what they want to believe. Point out that it is a new thing in hypnosis that can make an immoral person pure, a thief honest and a criminal go straight! In the final analysis no one can argue with experience—that's why a Christian's testimony to the changing power of Jesus Christ is so effective. Share the changes that have taken place in your own life since you came to know Jesus Christ. Three things should be emphasized: (1) the kind of life you lived prior to your conversion; (2) how you came to know Jesus Christ and accepted him as your Lord and Saviour; and (3) specific evidence of the change he has made in your life since you came to know him.

Bible References

There is no God else beside me; a just God and a Saviour; there is none beside me.

(Is 45:21)

A just weight and balance are the Lord's: all the weights of the bag are his work.

(Prov 16:11)

Good and upright is the Lord: therefore will he teach sinners in the way.

(Ps 25:8)

Lift up your eyes on high, and behold who hath created these things.

(Is 40:26)

The heavens declare the glory of God; and the firmament showeth his handywork.

(Ps 19:1)

We may be sure that all this will be taken into account in the day of true judgment, when God will judge men's secret lives by Christ Jesus, as my gospel plainly states.

(Rom 2:16 PHILLIPS)

What about the heathen?

Although the Bible does not tell us in precise detail how God will deal with this class of people, there are a number of scriptural facts which enable us to come to some definite conclusions. (1) God is just. All the evidence of the Bible shows that God will always act in harmony with his character, which is just and good (Gen 18:25). (2) The evidence of a Creator is seen in creation (Rom 1:19–20). For those who want to see, the evidence of God's existence is clearly displayed in the material universe. (3) No person will be condemned for rejecting Jesus Christ, of whom he has never heard, but for the violation of his own moral standards (Rom 2:12–16; Jn 1:4–5). (4) If a person responds to the light he has, and seeks God, then God will, in some way, enable him to hear of Jesus Christ (Jer 29:13; Mt 7:7–11). Show the person asking this question that there is no doubt what will happen to the person who has heard the gospel and rejected it. Sometimes a person will raise this question in order to divert attention away from any personal sense of conviction he may be feeling about the demands of Christianity. This fact needs to be presented to the person lovingly and gently. Terminate the discussion by focusing on this truth: God being just and righteous will bring all things to a satisfactory conclusion. The important issue you should be thinking of at this moment is what *you* are going to do about the matter of *your* relationship with Jesus Christ.

Bible References

All scripture is given by inspiration of God, and is profitable...

(2 Tim 3:16)

Holy men of God spake as they were moved by the Holy Spirit.

(2 Pet 1:21)

Sanctify them through thy truth: thy word is truth.

(Jn 17:17)

Then said the Lord...I will hasten my word to perform it.

(Jer 1:12)

Then shall ye know that I the Lord have spoken it, and performed it.

(Ezek 37:14)

O taste and see that the Lord is good.

(Ps 34:8)

Did not our hearts glow within us while he was talking to us on the road, and opened the scriptures to us?

(Lk 24:32 Berkeley Version)

The word of our God shall stand for ever.

(Is 40:8)

The Bible is full of errors

Ask the person what particular error he has in mind. Nine times out of ten a person who makes this statement does so because he has heard someone else say that the Bible is full of contradictions, but has not gone on to research for himself. If the person is unable to come up with a specific example, don't engage in ridicule. Under no circumstances should you make fun of anyone or attempt to make them look foolish. This approach proves counter-productive anyway. Share your own personal testimony of how reliable and accurate you have found Christ's promise of peace, pardon and security in your own life and experience. Point out that the promise Jesus made, 'My peace I give unto you' (Jn 14:27) is something that you have proved personally since you came to know him as your Lord and Saviour. Think up other examples of promises Christ made which you have personally proved. If on the other hand the person does come up with an apparent contradiction, and you don't have an immediate answer, don't panic but simply say, 'I don't have the answer to your question at the moment, but I'll be delighted to look it up and give you the answer later.' The Bible does contain some apparent contradictions, but there are satisfactory answers to every one of these. Almost any Christian bookshop will direct you to the books you ought to study which deal with the apparent contradictions of Scripture. *Difficulties in the Bible* by R. A. Torrey (Moody Press) is an excellent book to study, and although written in the early part of this century it speaks to the issues with great clarity.

Bible References

For thou wilt not leave my soul in hell; neither wilt thou suffer thine Holy One to see corruption.

(Ps 16:10)

And the third day he shall rise again.

(Mt 20:19)

Ye seek Jesus of Nazareth, which was crucified: he is risen; he is not here.

(Mk 16:6)

Afterward he appeared unto the eleven as they sat at meat, and upbraided them with their unbelief... because they believed not them which had seen him after he was risen.

(Mk 16:14)

For Christ also hath once suffered for sins, the just for the unjust, that he might bring us to God, being put to death in the flesh, but quickened by the Spirit.

(1 Pet 3:18)

The Son of man must suffer many things, and be rejected... and be slain, and be raised the third day.

(Lk 9:22)

Did Christ really rise from the dead?

The greatest miracle in the Bible is the miracle of the resurrection. This is why so many stumble over it and find it beyond belief. Some of the explanations given for Christ's resurrection make more demands on the human mind than the actual account itself. Some maintain, for example, that it was not the real body of Jesus which rose from the dead, but a ghost. It is a new thing in ghost stories which turns cowardly disciples into flaming evangelists! Others claim the disciples were so deluded that they merely *fancied* Christ had risen from the dead. The truth is that the disciples were altogether removed from the sort of mood that dreams up illusion, for instead of being excited after Jesus' death they were stunned by sorrow. Another theory is that the enemies of Christ broke into the tomb and stole the body of Jesus under cover of darkness. If this was so, than all the enemies of Christ had to do to disprove the resurrection was to produce the body. They did not, of course, because they could not. A final theory claims that the friends of Christ rifled the tomb and removed the corpse. But how could those frightened disciples overpower Roman guards, break Caesar's seal, and then foist upon mankind a wicked fraud? Such a theory does not fit the facts; neither does it satisfy human reason.

Bible References

In the beginning God....

(Gen 1:1)

The fool hath said in his heart, There is no God.

(Ps 14:1)

Who is this that darkeneth counsel by words without knowledge?...Where wast thou when I laid the foundations of the earth?

(Job 38:2, 4)

For the truth about God is known...instinctively. God has put this knowledge in their hearts. Since earliest times men have seen the earth and sky and all God made, and have known of his existence and great eternal power. So they will have no excuse.

(Rom 1:19–20 TLB)

O Lord my God, many and many a time you have done great miracles for us, and we are ever in your thoughts. Who else can do such glorious things? No one else can be compared with you. There isn't time to tell of all your wonderful deeds.

(Ps 40:5 TLB)

How can miracles be possible?

You must consider very carefully what lies behind this question, or else you will waste a good deal of time discussing issues such as 'Did Christ actually walk on the water?' or 'How could he feed five thousand people with only five loaves and two fishes?' The real issue behind this question is whether or not God exists, and the questioner is really having a problem not so much with miracles but with the fact of the existence of God. If God exists, then by definition he is all-powerful, and anyone believing in the existence of God will have no problem with accepting the miraculous. There are many arguments you can present for the existence of God, but the most telling is what is known as the argument from design. Put your wristwatch (or borrow one if you don't possess one) into the hands of the questioner and say, 'How long do you think it would take for that wristwatch to come together of its own accord?' You can proceed from there to show that a design needs a designer, and in the same way an orderly creation must, of necessity, have a Creator. Point out that, in fact, the Creator came to this earth two thousand years ago in the form of Jesus Christ to show us what he was like. Explain then that the only way to know God is through his Son, Jesus Christ.

Bible References

And we know that all things work together for good to them that love God, to them who are the called according to his purpose. For whom he did foreknow, he also did predestinate to be conformed to the image of his son.
(Rom 8:28–29)

My thoughts are not your thoughts, neither are your ways my ways, saith the Lord. For as the heavens are higher than the earth, so are my ways higher than your ways, and my thoughts than your thoughts.
(Is 55:8–9)

He restoreth my soul.... Yea, though I walk through the valley of the shadow of death...thou art with me.
(Ps 23:3–4)

And though...worms destroy this body, yet in my flesh shall I see God.
(Job 19:26)

I will restore to you the years that the locust hath eaten.
(Joel 2:25)

Shall not the Judge of all the earth do right?
(Gen 18:25)

Why does God allow so much suffering?

Pain, accidents, death, natural tragedies, etc. raise questions that cause some people a great deal of personal anguish. In the beginning God created a perfect world, but sin quickly damaged its potential and brought disruption to all parts of God's universe. Because of the nature of the universe, sin and suffering spread to affect life in all its various forms. To those who say, 'Why doesn't God just stamp out evil?' ask this question: 'If at midnight tonight, God decreed that all evil would be stamped out of the universe, how many of us would be here at 12:01?' God could obliterate all evil and suffering in the world by one single stroke, but all that that would prove is how much bigger and stronger he is. Instead he has allowed it to remain, in order to demonstrate not merely the attribute of power but those of wisdom and grace, and how these can work through evil and suffering to glorify his name. God does not, however, ask us to face evil and suffering without having first faced it himself. This he did on the cross, and through that cross he now provides us with the grace and power not only to face all evil and suffering, but to use it in deepening our sensitivity to life and making our characters into the image of Jesus Christ (Rom 8:28–29). The only solution to evil and suffering is to become a Christian, for then you receive the power and insight to turn everything to good.

The following books will help you to further develop your counselling ministry:

A Friend in Need by Selwyn Hughes (Kingsway Publications).
Christian Counselling by Gary Collins (Word UK).
Competent to Counsel by Jay Adams (Presbyterian and Reformed Publishing Company).
Restoring the Image by Roger Hurding (Paternoster Press).
Listening: A Christian's Guide to Loving Relationships by Norman Wakefield (Word UK).
Basic Principles of Biblical Counseling by Lawrence J. Crabb (Zondervan).
Know Why You Believe by Paul Little (Scripture Union).
Who Cares? by Evelyn Peterson (Paternoster Press).
The Christian's Handbook of Psychiatry by Quentin Hyder (Spire Books).
Telling Yourself the Truth by William Backus and Marie Chapman (Bethany).
Happiness is a Choice by Frank B. Minirth and Paul D. Meir (Baker).
Overcoming Hurts and Anger by Dwight L. Carson (Harvest House).